# leaving traces

mary pargeter

GB Publishing.org

All rights reserved. No part of this book may be reproduced or transmitted in any form by any means, electronic or mechanical, including photocopying, recording, or by any information storage and retrieval system without written permission of the publisher, except where permitted by law.

First published 2018 by GBP
GB Publishing.org

Copyright ©2018 Mary Pargeter
All rights reserved

ISBN: 978-1-912576-24-1 (hardback)
978-1-912576-25-8 (paperback)
978-1-912576-26-5 (eBook)
978-1-912576-27-2 (kindle)

A catalogue record of this book
is available from the British Library

Cover design ©2018 Mary Pargeter Design

*Cover inset photograph:*
*Mary aged 6 with brother*
*Edward, 8, at Hayling Island*

GB Publishing.org
www.gbpublishing.co.uk

# beginnings

3 white owl at dusk
4 brook farm
5 elemental
6 moon in my window
7 nothing answers
8 the laying on of hands

# recalling

13 the boots
14 tracing James Brody
15 the National Archives
16 beware! hot!
17 the closeness
18 the confrontation
19 maybe the man I should have married

# endings

23 legacy
24 no chance to say goodbye
25 suddenly in autumn
26 death eclipses everything
27 ashes to ashes
28 unresolved issues
29 final meeting
30 the reaper

31 the edge of death
32 last visit
33 boxed ashes
34 when all this is over
36 decline
37 funeral for a man of figures
38 spring sunset
39 across the field at summer sunset

## the bright side

43 the Christmas angel
44 the lion returns
45 after you left, Mum
46 schooldays with Brynids
49 now we are old
50 little Gwen
52 Cuba or Clacton?
54 initiation into intelligentsia
56 not naff enough
58 you can't beat Kent
60 man up, girl

## appendix

65 biography
69 review by Agnes Meadows, poet
75 other poetry by Mary Pargeter

beginnings

### white owl at dusk

Here I was born,
this downland hilltop,
the plunging valley, open skies,
the lane where strangers rarely come,
and where, over the field,
Northwards, the white owl flies
each evening at dusk across
the few cottages.

Clearly remembered,
the haunted atmosphere,
the silent hamlet at
summer day's end.
A timeless, centuries old quiet.
The village fool, indolent on a gate,
gazing across a dimming field.
Mysterious, the captured
silence and evening gloom,
supernatural in the darkening light,
belonging to a different time.

### brook farm

So this is where you played.
This shaded glade, sun-stippled beneath
the willow canopy at the water's edge.

A flash of fleeting shadow ghosts,
children, misty grey in the brook,
your phantom form, face turned, smiling.

Vanished small feet on the stone flags
down into broad pebbled shallows
where fingers dip in light-rippled water.

And beside the bordering path, the farm,
mellowed and creepered, age-worn brick
warmed by the afternoon sun.

Upstairs at a peeled-paint window, you,
orphan child, lean from the casement,
smocked girls calling from apple boughs.
Still, now, another season's fruit gathered below.

And behind, across these very fields, faintly,
a distant meandering group, the young widow's
children, sent to call in the cows.

**elemental**

This strangeness at the hurricane's edge,
    the sky flat steel,
processing torn fragments of pallid cloud
    across a pewtered light,
The sun turned red by Sahara sand.
    The trees are speaking,
stirring, sound on shivering sound,
    distant high,
sweeping there, whispering here.
    The silvery trembling
telling of memory and the passing of time.

**moon in my window**

White cold and climbing, the incandescent disc
Lights silent, ragged, westborne clouds across its face,
Scudding across the night sky and
Smiling with its seas like a pearl button.

Rain falls in a muffled myriad of tapping and dripping,
An orchestra of drops and eddies randomly patter and ripple.
I lie awake, mind still with empty spaces, the
Pale window ajar in sheet grey darkness as sounds trickle.

What madness is this, the universe stretching incomprehensible
And who made the rules?
Recalling decisions lightly taken, the gravity of effect,
How little it matters.

## nothing answers

From the pulpit, far over pews,
    the nave's high span and up to arches,
the chancel's void, above the altar,
    in space rebounding, light and fleeting,
Words, thin as air. I reach to grasp what is not there.
    There is no substance. There is no answer.
Yet sometimes, somewhere, unannounced,
    a sign of mysterious significance.

### the laying on of hands

The organ resounds in peels and chords
And from the vestry, clothed in
Cassocks flowing white, the clergy and
Golden-clad bishop assemble in splendour,
Processing as notes tumble and roar.
*'Peace be with you. And also with you.'*
A language of beauty these sacred sequences.
*'Over water the Holy Spirit moved*
*In the Beginning of Creation.'*
Fingers dip in sanctified water.
Kneeling submissive for laying of hands.
*'Confirm O Lord your servant with your Holy Spirit'.*
Hands press lightly as, unforeseen,
Swiftly rippling, waving down spine, a
Chainlink sensation, disturbing each bone.
Spiritual or physical – some power performs.
Annointed with oil, silky on forehead,
Perfumed, aromatic, exotic and holy.
This mystical ritual, ancient, medieval,
Anachronistic, yet still of our time.
*'God has delivered us from the dominion of darkness.*
*Shine as a light in the world.'*
The organ spills thunderous as candles are lighted,
While shielding his flame the richly robed bishop,
A lettered sophisticate with velvety voice
*'When you wane'*, he purrs
*'When His Presence fades, then light this candle.'*
A confident message confirming belief.
This resplendent prelate with mitre and crook,
Educated, embroidered, who
Channels strange power.

recalling

**the boots**

I brought my boots down from the loft
Covered in decades of grime,
Leather dull with dust,
Buckles congealed with dirt.
Cream and polish shone away the interval,
Spray loosened the zips till they ran.
The tag broken, recalled fingers
Pulling past jagged notches over jeans.
Lifted the jacket from the cupboard's recess,
Leather mouldy with confinement.
Slipped it on, tight, unfastenable.
Hands into zipped pockets find badges,
TT emblems in my palm.
The sudden memory stares back,
Motorway rain, his beautiful hair.
And here I am in an unexpected
Surprise of the past.
Many years I stood in these boots,
Half a century old, in cafes and car parks,
Racetracks and roadsides,
Fit for purpose above rainsoaked
Tarmac or muddy woodland paths.
Forget I look like mutton dressed as lamb,
I know this.

### tracing James Brody

I could almost fall for you, James Brody.
Turn-of-the-century Irish immigrant,
Gaelic-speaking son of
Illiterate, ten-souls-to-three-rooms
Catholic family, County Donegal,
Come to build the railways
Through countryside to the West.
Itinerant engine driver, passing,
Deflowering the village girl
For love or lust... but wedding.
Barely three months till
Witnessed on her death certificate,
My mother's birth, same date, same hand.
      'James Brody.
   Widower of deceased
     Present at the death'
Last seen cycling from the village,
Leaving no trace.

## the National Archives

It's like you have been waiting for me
To come, to understand,
To approach this academic archive of
Grey slab and slate stretching between a
Spring blue sky and fountain-flecked lake.
Catalogued in this repository of
Tragedy and triumph, your story
Inside a bulky manilla folder,
Page after page of men,
Your name, dates and list.
Nineteen forty-two to five,
Changi, Ban Pong, Chunkai,
Kamburi, Nong Pladuc. Camps on the
Burma Railway, Death Railway.

I read the testimonies.
Disease, dysentry, diptheria,
Cholera, beri-beri, malaria,
Ulcers, amputations, improvisations.
No medicines, nutrition,
Slave labour, starvation,
Monsoons, flood, mud,
Mosquitoes, lice, bugs.
Marched, worked to death.
Sick forced from bed,
Beatings, punishments.
The litany too long to retain.
On this flimsy dusty-pink
Liberation Questionnaire,
Your neat handwritten replies.
It has taken me this long.
It is as if you are watching.

**beware! hot!**

Tsssssssst! Hot!
Fingers-burnt hot
Sparks flying, jangling hot
Head-spinning, tongue-tying hot
Crackling blind hot
Sightless hot
I can't see you hot.
Too hot to handle hot
Hell in paradise hot
Beware! Hot!

**the closeness**

The closeness, I miss the closeness.
To wake and climb out to make tea,
Put on worn slippers and ragged dressing gown,
Lean back in bed, twittering mindlessly
About trivial concerns that build with speaking,
While you lie senseless, the
Walnut tree framed in the window
Changing with the seasons.

Paddle about, run the bath and step in first.
While you stand shaving, I chatter and splash.
Lying in second-hand bathwater
You look up smiling from the warmth
As I dry my scarred legs by your face.

Drive to the same Saturday night pub
In rain, even flood, frost, even snow,
With fresh washed hair and warm feet in clean socks
As we settle into our usual table,
Talk of the week gone and things to come.

To put my hand in at the car window as you leave
Ready for kissing, and you take it and
Blow a kiss and wave all the way out of sight.
Every time. The closeness,
I miss the closeness.

### the confrontation

Why is she walking down the path
From your front door locked with her key?
This is the path you and I
Go to places from and come home to.

Why is she getting into my seat?
That's the car we bought at auction on a whim
And wondered what you'd bought.
That's my seat, where I put my feet on the dash
To relieve my aching legs.

Why is she asking me if we do anything together?
She knows nothing. Why am I answering?
Why am I discussing our life with this stranger?
Justifying the years we have shared
With this self-styled counsellor?

Why are you defending her against me?
You stand against me talking of your life together
I knew nothing of.
Why are you looking at me with contempt
And asking me if I have finished?
Like nothing mattered.

### maybe the man I should have married

What is this after half a century?
Unexpectedly from the envelope
An unseen black and white photo.
You and I on a steely cold race day
Sitting before a bank of brambles,
Muffled in the grey murk, holding
Thin white triangular sandwiches,
Plastic teacups at our feet.

The simple Sixties style of
Frugality and freedom. You facing
The camera, the dark good looks.
A surprise connection softly
Penetrating direct from the print.
Seeing your gentle smile
Came the dawning that maybe
You were the man I should have married,
Just as my aunt always said,
Chastising my stupidity.

You wore your heart on your sleeve,
Handwriting the poem, forever remembered,
'Tread softly because you tread on my dreams'
And bringing white lilies.
I want to marry a farmer I had said.
We can do that, the simple reply.
Your diffidence disguising a
Steady determination.
I hear you are sailing round the world.
My kind of man.
My kind of mistake.

endings

**legacy**

Lift the shroud and
Let me see her face,
Touch the cold cheek.
Mother, you kept your secret,
Deserving silence. The legacy,
Strengthening with time,
Kindness sometimes wiser than truth,
Gentleness stronger than force.
I don't know the answers
Though I keep asking.
Everything founders, falters.
But this endures.

*also*

**no chance to say goodbye**

>   I didn't know
> when you sat in my wingchair
>   it would be for the last time.
> My birthday. You gave me the painting
> of my house, thought the roof was slightly wrong,
> but it would look lovely on that wall.
> It hangs there now.

>   I didn't know
> when we picked vegetables with the children
>   it would be for the last time.
> You carried the raspberry canes away,
> and there already planted, the first time
> I returned to your home – after you died.
> I brought the last harvest in today,
> the late sun golden and vivid in your absence.

>   I didn't know
> when I heard your voice in the next room
>   it would be for the last time.
> So casually was I aware.
> But I knew how it would be.
> You nearly died once. I knelt and
> prayed you would make it through the night.

>   I didn't know
> when you walked up the path and
> sat in the garden swing with a cup of tea
>   it would be for the last time.
> Just snatched away.
> No time to help. No time for thanks.

## suddenly in autumn

The apples lay where they fell.
    Untouched.
Leaves scattered.
    Unmoved.
Always immaculate, it is clear that
You have not, will not, return.
A shirt placed by your hands
On the chair back.
    Unremoved.
Washing left hanging damp, now dry.
I fold the creased clothes, fabric
Soft and limp, one last time.
Within a cupboard shirts hang,
Crisp and ordered.
    Your home.
So much of you with its
Fine fabrics and tasteful, tidy rooms.
And through the picture window, the
Landscaped garden, leaves strewn.
There, tucked together on the sideboard,
Tickets for dates missed, bookings
Where you never showed.
The life you planned and well deserved.
    This house is full of you.
You should be here, have had more time.

### death eclipses everything

Medieval and mystical,
The sombre organ, the
Priest's dour incantation
And tolling bell striking in
Sonorous symmetry.
Unsteadily the raised coffin
Proceeds into church darkness,
Behind, the grieving family,
Unapproachable with
Spiritual ascension.
I climb the pulpit,
Step after inevitable step,
In the silence which
My voice alone will break.
Nothing matters today.
All else is deadened.
Death is paramount.

You looked across from the
Lychgate into the hearse,
Into the shaded interior.
I had forgotten you might be there.
It didn't matter.
Death eclipses everything.
She stood by your side,
Rather plain, rather ordinary.
Quizzical, you looked at me,
Not longingly, not regretfully
But curious.
Unexpectedly, I met your gaze,
Held for a long moment.
For a still moment, history
Connected. Time halted for the
Passing of an instant.
You looked away. Transient.
The black cortege moved off.

**ashes to ashes**

Tipped into a cube of earth
in a cloud of white dust.
Tumbling mix, body and bone,
mingling ash, ash of teeth, ash of ankle,
ash of passion, ash of anguish.
Bone white ashes, damaged ashes,
sent away from home ashes,
three children and barely twenty ashes,
money's tight ashes, ash of athlete,
business ashes, five star ashes,
ash of operations,
too early, too late ashes.
Ashes that lie alone. Goodbye ashes.
Ash of genes, feet from your ash
half circle the earth's waiting recess,
brown shoes, shiny shoes,
fashion shoes, pointed shoes,
high heel shoes.
In the small brown square
white ash luminescent in its clay cube
and a final dark covering.

# *also*

### unresolved issues

I wish I could come and see you
In your house by the sea.
Drive there now
On a winter Sunday,
Say can we resolve this,
Explain and go our ways.
See the things you chose
In your house by the sea.
You asked. But I never came.
The cut too deep.
Not now. When
I should have come
In your living time.
Not after you lay dead
Overnight alone
In your house by the sea
Among the things you chose.

I should have forgiven.
The church told me.
A warning only days before.
Forgive. Forgive.
I didn't listen.
The door has closed.
And as I write, a
Clatter from upstairs.
A brass chain has fallen.
I hear that. You have come.
I forgive you, if you forgive me.
Not enough.
I forgive unconditionally.
You can leave now. You can go.
Move on to wherever you are going.

### final meeting

And as we travelled, the
Morning sky pale lit with Spring,
Budded daffodils on green banks,
As the Sussex brick flashes by,
While you lie inert, waiting,
Your pallored face dark beneath the lid.
As fields sweep by,
And the Downs glide by.
And as we travelled, searching,
You are carried, chauffeured to
Our final meeting by
Sombre strangers buttoned in dark coats.
And now the cortege, black, shiny, and
Shocking, and inside You
In Sunday best,
Flowered and wreathed,
Ready for burial. The strangeness
Electric in the daylight.

### the reaper

Black it comes,
Sucking from its cloaked hiding
Wrapping its evil, like a leaden grip,
Carrying its deadly story,
Enfeebling and felling.
No more and no matter.
Soon, quite soon this will be.
And voices may sing the
Old hymns we loved as the
Organ pipes our history.
Loss and acceptance and
The coming to terms.
Try to grasp as I may,
Life and death hover elusive
At the edge of seeing,
Thinly penetrating the
Naked truth, the confusion
Of living and dying. Exposed,
Truth stands awesome and
Barechested at death,
Drawing back his robes,
Steadily watching near death and dying.

# also

### the edge of death

And finally here in this darkened room,
This prepared half-lit sepulchre where
Soft music quietens the surreal space,
Like a slip of a gasping girl you lie,
A black-clad priest incanting absolution in
Ancient supplication, and anointing holy oil
While slight shoulders heave, snatching breath
In repetitive expelled rhythm.
And so the panting breath-beat,
Hour by hour to nightime stillness,
Shallower, lighter, slower.
Face death-shaped, the skull-curve
Of cheek and dropped jaw,
Head back, skin stretched ashen,
Open mouth taut.

But, now, something has changed.
Strange, more urgent, more
Intense this aura. I beckon.
Nurses warn, bent still, watch and listen.
Clearly the very edge of death.
Lighter, slower. Then in a wave,
Like a wash across your face,
Expression softening, lines fade.
The merest glimpse of a smile as if,
Surprised, in wonderment, a scene delights.
So long the wait to one tiny last breath.
Now like a windswept girl you lie,
Pillowed black hair glossy in folds
About the carved bone structure and
Lovely sculptured face.

**last visit**

You were given the term.
Less, and too soon I sit
Bemused beside your coffin,
Inside, your lifeless frame,
Chest still as stone
Beneath white satin gown,
Dead roses clasped in folded hands,
As a girl at confirmation.
A decaying husk,
Face frozen in expression
I hardly know.
A shaded parlour where
Three candles burn in the
Eerie dim light.

### boxed ashes

I placed the box on the chair
Where once you sat,
Perfumed and jewelled,
To meet again your lost love,
The one who broke your heart.
Indents of stilettoes still
Mark the wooden floor.
A sedentary box where once
Your vital body, animated by
Sarcasm and the scorn of quick wit,
Lived and breathed and moved.
A simple static box, inside the
Residue of choice and chance,
The sum of your sad story.

### when all this is over

When all this is over
I shall phone you up,
discuss the funeral,
who was there,
what was worn,
identify mourners
and how we've all aged.

Except you won't answer.

When all this is over
I shall come for a pizza.
The doorbell will ring,
you'll hand me the box,
pour the red wine,
lie on the sofa. Talk of
lost loves. I'd come

Except you won't be there.

When all this is over a
Christmas card will come,
expected as normal
with the usual greeting,
and put on the windowsill
along with the others.

Except it won't arrive.

When all this is over
you'll be back in the garden,
clearing for winter,
preparing for spring,
growing, planting
for next year's colour.

Except they won't bloom.

When all this is over
something will remind me.
Discover a photo, a
gift that you gave me.
Remember the good times
pictured in memory

For there you will be.

*also*

### decline

Pictured in the order of service
In clipped-waist wedding dress of lace,
Beneath stiffened hem, gazelle-like ankles,
And beaming with virginal purity
From beneath a profusion of white net.
I wish I had been like that.
But all that is done cannot be undone.
And towards your life together,
Global and exotic, with the husband
Who sent this day, defying superstition,
His note of love and thanks,
Long before alcoholism, his
Gambling that drove you to scrimp.

But not in these pictures.
A class act in your post-war pencil-thin
Costume, gloved and hatted,
The chic head now static, grey straggle
Coiffeured in the coffin,
Wracked brain stilled. The zest
Turned to a mind wasted.
'We'll meet again', the strain as if you,
Singing from beyond the grave,
Have left the leaving trace of you.
And in the graveyard, carpeted with
Decaying petal blossom, like you,
From springlike to blasted,
Joyful to destroyed.
I throw down dust onto your nameplate.
Fine sprinkling dust.
Dust onto the friendship
And its ending.

## funeral for a man of figures

Indeed, my participation in The World of Work ended.
My man of figures, taxes and incomprehensible year ends
Laid in his casket, columns, additions, deductions frozen,
Halted, as he lived, in a capsule of time
Circa nineteen hundred and ten, his home
A shrine to 'dear Mama', departed,
As custodian, her devoted bachelor son.
"Think of me, speak to me in the easy way
You always used", asks the faltering reading.
Picturing myself, younger, working prime,
Seated upon brocaded upholstery,
Amongst Edwardian carved furnishings,
Mahogany mouldings, patterned paper,
Lace antimaccasars, fringed pelmets,
Filigree-framed portraits and pastoral paintings,
Receipt-filled supermarket bags at feet,
Extracting cash analysis and self assessment forms
In this visual bombardment of ornament,
Sipping scented tea from fine china cups,
Two biscuits placed on matching side plate,
Confused by profits, percentages and payments.
Finally, closing accounts to retirement,
A sobering, disturbing rite of passage.
Your death at ninety-four finalising the
Gentile, perennial pattern of this
Singular, original timewarp.
Another nail in the coffin, you could say.

**spring sunset**

A pale springtime sun sets in a white blurred ball of
Dazzling pure light, the trees dappled with
Lemon green freshness against their boned structure.
Apple blossom buds, baby pink and white in their simplicity.
Lovely, the lilac has returned with its towered blooms,
And the first bees on the rosemary.
The pink camelia, frost touched, dropped in a carpet of decay.
Dry, dusty lavender new cushions of tender velvet softness,
Bright primroses, fresh as milk, light the shadows.
Exhuberant and plush, all is thrusting to fullness with the
Bursting of Spring, while calling across the gardens from tree to tree
Chirp and chirrup and whistle and trill

As the sun sinks in a blaze.

### across the field at summer sunset

The western sky stretches in an expanse of powder blue,
The horizon painted in thin strokes of cloud
Bleached by a low sun blazing white with intensity.
Crazy, swirling twists of mosquitoes dance above the tufted grass.
Captured in the flood of light, bloodsuckers hover vertically on
Orange whirling wings, translucent against the sunlight.
Across the stillness, a batting of pigeon's wings disturbs the quiet.
Now clouds flatten in an iridescent pink and ivory streaked band,
Here and there arching upwards, thrown by celestial wind
While the sun turns to gold, illuminating brick in a rich terracotta,
Saturating colour, light and shade in vivid contrast.

Suddenly, sunlight dissolves and a grey wash veils the garden as
Evening cools and colour slips away, ebbing and edging to pewter.

# the bright side

*'once you realise we are all mad life begins to make sense'*

### the Christmas angel

God has sent me here,
Perched atop this scrappy tree,
Precariously attached by
Little fingers which unbent me,
Pulled out my wings and,
Strapped me to the top branch,
Slightly skew-whiff so the
Room's at a bit of an angle.
I can hardly bear another
Christmas up here listening to
The arguments. My mission is
To represent the Christian faith,
Although there's precious
Little indication of that here.
It's nearly one o'clock and if the
Dinner isn't on the table soon
There'll be all hell let loose.
He's got a filthy temper
And the kids will cower.
They don't take a lot of notice of me,
Only the occasional glance, so I feel
I'm wasting my time symbolically
Professing the Love of God.
The radio plays the occasional
Christmas carol and mixed with the
Smell of sprouts it should be festive,
But there's a miserable atmosphere
Although Mum tries her best.
After the Queen's speech they'll be
Taking the presents off the tree and
I might get a bit wobbly but
With the help of God
I'll survive another year.

**the lion returns**

Down the nightime street,
on his head the newspaper
folded into a boat
to shield the rain, and
flapping round his shins,
trouser bottoms
shrunk from washing and
creased above giant
size thirteen plastic sandals
purchased cheap from
a Soho market.
My father, back from London,
returning from rehearsals
as the Lion opposite Androcles.

### after you left, Mum

I don't blame you for leaving,
You were a Saint,
But the place is neglected
And the food's terrible.

I've not left London yet
And the chips are on,
Saturated in lard rendered
From butcher's offcuts and
Dented with mouse footprints.
Displayed on laid table, the
Glutinous stew, squares of fat
Dyed green by processed peas.
His economy wartime creation
That puts the coal fire out.

Legs in the clothes airer
Propped against the armchair,
Waving and warming his top with the
Hairdryer, he sits incarcerated
And armed before the TV,
Aiming unsteadily at
Push buttons with a bamboo pole
Hacked from the garden jungle,
Where television tubes lie
Strewn in the undergrowth.

This weekend I shall heat up the
Boiler and mangle the sheets
And when he shouts for coffee
Tell him to get his own. I'm busy!
He doesn't answer back.
That's how to treat a bully.
I'm going to Cornwall soon to
Live in my van. I'm just going!

### schooldays with Brynids

Platforms and porters,
Coal fires in waiting rooms,
Ladies Room antics,
Pull-down train windows
And Ladies compartments,
Goldfinger, gardens and
Gabardined perverts.

Parapet bridge with
My shoe flying over.
Satchel emptied down
Mind-the-gap space.
Lying in hat racks,
Flying from hat racks
To unsurprised travellers.

Lying in ditches,
Smoking in ditches.
You moaning from
Goalmouth with
Hockey sticks flailing.
Sharing out sandwiches,
Dinner money saving,
Five Nelson or Consulate,
Fags a priority.

Creating our nicknames
For coolness and street cred.
Rolling up waistbands
To mini skirt level.
Berets abandoned,
Ties stuffed in pockets.

Adopting attitude with
Sneering dismissal.
Hammer horror movies
And journey home terrors.

Prized find in stream, the
Great Diving Water Beetle,
Poised in enamel bowl
Ready for striking a
Pitiful tadpole, and
Pickled by mistress.
Boredom in lessons,
Crossing off boxes on
Drawn-up term hourchart.

Houses unheated and
Furnished, unchanging.
Afternoon tea a strict
Formal laid table,
Waiting and timing
Controlled for no pleasure.

Sitting surveying, hunger unsated.
No asking till offered,
No speaking till asked.
'Can we get down?'
Timed to perfection.
'Can we get down, what?'
'Please', to tennis court garden.

Crusader camp tedium
You fighting off bully.
Prayers five times daily
Too much for us children.
Even glad to be home
And that's saying something.

Dressing-up clothes from
Cupboard on landing.
Slipping Irish accent
In our family creation.
Assassination announcement
By your father in bedroom.
Kennedy's dead, we all
Feel it's serious.

Seeing The Beatles,
No sound but the screaming.
The fence at the back where
We hoped we would meet them.
White-lipsticked, black-eyelined
And black plastic jackets.

The Stones in the town hall,
Third full, from the gallery.
Keith looking cool. He was
Always my favourite.
Hitchhiking home, car
Breakdown in woodland,
Running and picked up
By saviour of neighbour.

And so we continued our
Fruitless education.
A bind to our teachers,
No mark of distinction or
Prize for posterity,
No feted alumnae or
Proud lettered boards.
No plan for the future,
No sense at all really,
But making it plain
We knew everything
Worth knowing.

### now we are old

Let's not talk about men.
Let's talk of funerals,
What hymns were chosen,
And readings selected,
And teeth and treatments,
Pensions and pills,
Bad backs and bulges,
Surgical stockings and
Compression knickers.
Let's go ooh and aah and
Suck in sympathetically
And fill our boots with
Moaning and groaning.
Let's talk about what time
We went to bed and
What time we got up
And what we had for tea.
Let's not talk about men.

### little Gwen

Gwen, Gwennie, daughter of
Nanny Billie and PipPop,
Offspring of music-hall mother and
Military Major. Trim teenage dancer
Following family footsteps
Onto stage. A picture of
Glamour with innocence,
Sincerity and warmth,
Looking over your shoulder in
Fur and fashionable blonde set,
Pretty face aglow with brightness.

Wartime wedding night hotel room,
While the blitz raged, beside your
Childhood sweetheart, the wit, the
Convivial imbiber, in old age recalling,
His eyes distant with memory,
Melody reminding,
'Room One Hundred and Four'.
He dreaming of Hollywood,
You simply home.

Young bride installed above off-licence,
Where eccentrics appear from shop
Below, past boxed alcohol and life-sized
Sandeman's Sherry cut-out toreador
To the flat above for further indulgence.
Busy housewife chided by mother's
Gravelly lisp. 'Thsit down Gwen,
You muthst be made of cathst-iron.'

Fifties mother at gas ring
Between kitchenette's
Formica drop-leaf dresser and
Matching table, a neat figure in
Nifty cut-away shorts, melting
Cheese into baked beans for us
Children and, decades later,
Arriving gleeful, proffering
Heinz tin and cheddar wedge,
Girlishly giggling, husband
In fun collusion like the
Youngsters they remained.

'Look at the dear little thing!'
As a shaggy mongrel passes.
'Oh, look at the dear little thing!'
At an unappealing, gurgling baby.
Now in gown and furry slippers
With childlike worldliness at
Nearly one hundred, still the
Sparkling smile and
Ready, sharing laugh.
'Hello dear. What darling?
Yes. Anything dear.'

## Cuba or Clacton?

Ole! Look at me dancing!
I am sixty going on twenty
Striking a Salsa pose
Hands high, cellulite shuddering,
Thread veins prominent
Despite conker brown tan,
Breasts swaying beneath
Russet cleavage wrinkles.
Simulated maraca-shaking, tanned
Tubby-tummy partner mirroring my
Contrived but uncoordinated
Leg pattern with his twinkletoes
And sachaying off with his
Join-in gestures, false teeth flashing.
He's twenty too!
But it's all in the head this dancing.

Passing, lean and nervy, bald ex-skinhead,
Arms blue with over-tattooing and
Che Guevara chested image.
Yes, I am Che. Che, the hero.
Elderly Casanova, hair slicked back,
Pure white combed strands
Bright on overbronzed neck,
Inscrutable behind black pilot sunglasses,
Significant chained ring nestled golden
On broad coconut thatch chest.
Yes, I am still a cool geezer.
And you, inscribed James Lauren,
Dragoned and skulled,
Sprawled on stomach on poolside lounger
Proudly displaying a myriad of tattoo choices.

Bravo! come the cries to the badly
Entwined legs and unsteady footing,
Arms haphazardly waving,
And it's only mid-morning.
Is this Cuba or Clacton? Cha-cha-cha.
Yes, we still cut it. Still the main men.
These ageing dudes with their
Sunbaked, sundried, suncrinkled missus.
Look at us! Look at them.
Samba, Salsa, Mamba, Rumba
More Mojitos! Cuba Libres!

### initiation into intelligentsia

My foray into academia, the evening
Soirée of Greek literature amongst the
Intelligentsia, classics' scholars and dons.
In this exclusive, educated company,
My lack of learning exposed,
I recall entering Delhi airport hotel,
Dirty and diseased, like an urchin,
Filthy from backpacking. Here, the same
Sense of stepping straight from the street,
Realism colliding with refinement.

Summoned from chilled Chardonnay and
Contemporary canapés to lecture hall where
Experts on stage, with token woman panellist –
Supremely confident and bafflingly articulate –
Are cowed by her dominance.
Richly-expressive readings resonate while
The chairman lip-syncs to lyrics in
Paroxysms of delight, shaking his head in
Appreciative wonderment, language lapsing into
Latin while the audience collectively chuckles,
Reminding of their exalted understanding.

Empowered feminist from the auditorium:
"Should we read Ovid as he raped his lover's servant?"
I groan, audibly, catching my neighbour's attention
And, as this vein continues, shifting in irritation,
Then, startlingly from the stage, the chairman,
Smiling guilelessly: Would we rather be raped by Apollo
Or another Greek character, lost in the murmuring?
Is he joking? A daring, veiled retaliation?
Is this high sardonic humour of an elevated level?
Whatever, I like the cut of his jib.
Whoever they are, I'll have the main man, please.

And so to the mingling drinks reception.
I know I shall disappoint. First bore,
Then unsettle polite society.
I shall offend with politics and policies,
Gazes, and feet, will wander, save for
My dogged companion, an adolescent
Adopting me as some sort of oracle
Despite my denial of any knowledge,
Perhaps too young for discernment or
Causing discomfort to the middle classes.

Tipsy, temporary confidence propels me
Towards the gorgeous young barrister,
Oxford classics' graduate, who previously,
Probably to his regret, approached and,
Like some drunk in the pub, swaying stupidly,
"I have to tell you" I say, "I have to tell you.
This Me Too movement is a load of crap."
He doesn't reply, like most men, wary of
Opinions, passes and prosecutions.
"You have to live life. They will never be poets."

## not naff enough

When holidaying we choose naff
It's what we like, without a faff.
No bells and whistles and all that
Just a lot of basic tat.
Essex is the place for us,
Or so we thought, and no fuss.
Funfairs, fruit machines and chips
High heels, busts and Botox lips.

But Clacton's smartened up its act,
A disappointment, that's a fact.
Jaywick is a rare oasis,
Police car parked on permanent basis.
Along the coast Martello towers
Displaying our defensive powers
Showing Napoleon who's boss
'We're warning you, mate, just clear off.'

Southend boasts the longest pier
A mile to end – it rained I fear –
Plus after staggering quite a hike
Not a penny arcade in sight.
Canvey Island's Thirties' caff
Restored and painted, no longer naff.
Fish 'n chips now gentrified
Maybe sautéed, not even fried.
Estuary vista of sea and skies,
Merchant shipping and Thames tides.

Essex girls put us in shade.
Compared, we just don't make the grade.
Fake-tanned, false nails, groomed and smart
Tattooed, tight-trousered with touch of tart.
White van man's on the ball
Working for himself, an' all.
Self-reliant and self-employed
PAYE a state to avoid.
Better prospects he would forge
For himself, England and St George.

Even if they're on the fiddle
The countryside's a rural idyll.
Sweeping fields of arable crops,
Water, windfarms and nail shops.
History, a sense of place,
This isolated landmass race
Repelling boarders from the sea
'Oi, mate, don't mess with me.'

But I digress because of course
We came to find the best of worst.
Experience sometimes will deflate
Because we're sorry to relate
That it's not tacky, it's not rough
Essex is just not naff enough.

## you can't beat Kent

For quintessential seaside stay,
Short break, daytrip, holiday,
The Costa del Sol has sun and sand
But Kent is just so close at hand.

A treasure trove of such finesse
Margate, Dymchurch, Dungeness.
No pleasure-seeking pleb should waste
His benefit cheque in seeking more
Than chips and dodgems on its shore.

Degenerate Margate, what can compare
Now Dreamland's restored, and bracing air!
They say it's on the turn but some
May beg to differ – and will they come?

Broadstairs' bandstand after Sunday teas,
Brassband favourites, families,
Kids to grans, the crowd just stares,
Vacant gazes from rows of chairs.

Ramsgate's red disturbing hue
Creates a quite unsettling view,
The Victorians' bold attempt to render
An epitome of seaside splendour.
Now in view from its pretty dock,
A token sixties high-rise block.

The Isle of Sheppey and Sheerness,
Industrial godforsaken nothingness.
Despite the giant steelworks plant
'Work' appears proceeded by 'can't'.

Here obesity is no disgrace
What is there to do but stuff your face?
And everywhere the walking stick,
Surely they must be taking the mick.
Necessary perhaps to get about
As cameras could catch you out.

The council poster's pitiful aim
With languorous mermaid to proclaim
'Welcome to Sheerness', but farewell to all
For nobody's come here to call.

But despite the rain and lack of sun
Why not head South for seaside fun?
Stop and spend, do more than glance
From the M25 on the way to France.
So let's be helpful, it's time we went,
Let's all start driving down to Kent.

### man up, girl

Stuff political correctness
Be outspoken, let's be reckless.
Fragile snowflake generation
Of self-protection veneration,
Banter's just a bit of fun,
Battle of the sexes, never won.
Surely we can still distinguish
Without the risk that we extinguish
Harmless flirting, specially while young,
Seriousness is overdone.

Make the most of what you've got
While you have it, before the rot.
If dressing sexy gives satisfaction
Don't complain when there's reaction.
If what you wear provokes a rake
You can't have it and eat your cake.
Enjoy it now while you attract.
Men will be men, thank God for that.
Milk it now for what it's worth
Later on you'll feel the dearth.

Students blocking speakers' views
Only listening to what they choose.
It's worrying that they should fear
What they're too delicate to hear.
Who wants to live overprotected?
Common sense has been rejected.
Since when did students have say-so
Tutors unite – just say no.

Flashers weren't uncommon when
We just called them dirty old men.
Whistles received a grateful reception.
I suppose it's all about perception.
If being fancied causes objection
How does that compare to rejection?
Men have always chanced their luck
In the hope of a successful... outcome.
Not unknown wheedling, pawing
In the hope of finally scoring.

No-one said life would be easy
Men are nice and men are sleazy.
You think it's wrong, you think it's rude
But can you change this attitude?
Would you prefer, weak and limp,
An emasculated wimp?
I realise I'm behind the curve
And what I say could touch a nerve.
Ardent feminists may get cross
But I don't really give a toss.

Snowflakes melt when times get hard,
Just get savvy, be on guard.
Rape's of course a different matter
Can screw you up, lives can shatter,
But for goodness sake get a perspective
On this precious, self-righteous invective.
So what if sexual advances are rife
Man up, girl, that is life.

# appendix

# biography

English poet Mary Pargeter was born in 1948 at the family home in Newton Valence, a tiny hamlet in Hampshire. Her idyllic childhood was spent running free in the countryside near Selborne, that evocative landscape which is now part of the South Downs National Park.

Village children walked two miles across fields to the local primary school where her mother was a teacher. Her father – an eccentric radio physicist who ruled the family – ran a market garden, having retired as a regular soldier from the army after four years in a Japanese prisoner of war camp.

When the family moved to suburban Surrey in 1955, much to Mary's dismay, trees and greenery were replaced by pavements and streetlights.

In the 1960s, being the ideal age to experience the groundbreaking youth culture, she and friends immersed themselves in that exciting and iconoclastic era.

No doubt influenced by her father who, while living in India in the 1920s and 30s was a keen motorcyclist and aviator, she rode motorbikes and later obtained a pilot's licence.

Studying art, she became a freelance graphic designer from which she recently retired.
In her early 20s both parents died, and more recently her brother and sister.

*traces from*

Mum and sister 1943

Dad 1927

From left: brother, myself, sister

Home and market garden
Newton Valence, Hampshire

Flying, Booker Airfield, High Wycombe 1982

*he past*

With brother, Hayling Island 1954

Sally the dog, 1962

Whitenose the cat, 1958

Motorcyling 1969

# review

*by Agnes Meadows, Poet*

"*Leaving Traces*" is Mary Pargeter's second collection, and one which fully embraces life's tragedies, sorrows and regrets, as well as some of the things that amuse or remind us of nature's bounty. It is a collection packed with poignant, emotional images that haunt, staying with you long after you've read the poems.

Evocative and nostalgic are words that spring to mind over and over again when reading Mary's exquisitely crafted collection. The common thread linking each of its four parts is sadness for what was once replete with life and promise, but which has now passed, as expressed in the closing lines of '*Elemental*'

*'The silvery trembling*
*telling of memory and the passing of time.'*

There is a ghost-like quality about this writing, as if each word and phrase is a thread in the writer's rich tapestry of years and memories, the past an ever-present but remote reality, all of it imbued with elemental magic and the mystery of the natural world.

In '*Recalling*' Mary writes with real regret about the ending of a relationship, a regret containing barely suppressed outrage and restrained anger at her abandonment and what came after. '*The Confrontation*' takes a closer look at this desertion, finishing with a few succinct, tight-lipped questions that will never be answered:

*'Why are you defending her against me?*
*You stand against me talking of your life together*
*I knew nothing of.*
*Why are you looking at me with contempt*
*And asking me if I have finished?*
*Like nothing mattered.'*

Ouch!

The section closes with a poetic look at '*Maybe the man I should have married*', commenting it was '*My kind of man. My kind of mistake.*' All of us who have been wounded by the end of a marriage or relationship will identify with what is being expressed here.

There's more anger in '*Endings*', which probes the aching tooth of the past again and again, the dead relationship that has clearly left a plethora of wounds, the scar-tissue of pain, the death of a once-beloved someone explored painfully in '*Death Eclipses Everything*' and '*Ashes to Ashes*', which looks at a life-time shared, where each family milestone is reduced to a plethora of ashes.

*'Bone white ashes, damaged ashes,
sent away from home ashes,
three children and barely twenty ashes,
money's tight ashes, ash of athlete...'*

As the collection unfolds, regret for times past is amplified, the memories of relationships and friendships frozen in the maelstrom of life and its passage, everything becoming pale and spectral.

In *'When all this is over'* the pain of regret for what has been lost reaches an aching crescendo in the realisation that the death of the beloved one cannot be reversed except in hopeful imagination.

*'When all this is over
something will remind me.
Discover a photo, a
gift that you gave me.
Remember the good times
pictured in memory
For there you will be.'*

In this and subsequent poems, the minutiae of life are highlighted, for they contain all those elements which inspire both the greatest regrets and most nostalgic recollections, and are highlighted in carefully chosen words/ pictures. Again, this is something most readers will be able to relate to and identify with.

The collection continues with another section entitled '*the bright side – once you realise we are all mad, life begins to make sense*'.

This displays a more humorous side to Mary's work, with the usual biting observations, although not necessarily happy ones. '*The Christmas Angel*' is a list poem told from the point of view of the angel at the top of the Christmas tree, who witnesses the usual highs and lows of Christmas day in the average household.

*'I can hardly bear another*
*Christmas up here listening to*
*The arguments. My mission is*
*To represent the Christian faith,*
*Although there's precious*
*Little indication of that here.'*

How very true! Been there a dozen times at least!

'*Schooldays with Brynids*' catalogues youthful sins, joys, and indiscretions, its staccato rhythmic phrasing adding to the quickening passage of remembrance of younger days, gathering momentum to a smiling conclusion.

The section closes with a short series of pieces that have broken into mischievous rhyming, an excellent way to end what might otherwise be an overly nostalgic/melancholy collection. '*Not naff enough*' is another list, taking a witty look at holidaying in Essex.

*'When holidaying we choose naff*
*It's what we like, without a faff.*
*No bells and whistles and all that*
*Just a lot of basic tat.*
*Essex is the place for us,*
*Or so we thought, and no fuss.*
*Funfairs, fruit machines and chips*
*High heels, busts and Botox lips.'*

Love it!!

Ultimately, I loved the whole collection because, despite its often painful and nostalgic themes, it was beautifully written by a poet who has clearly taken a great deal of time and thought to fine-tune each memory, real or imagined, allowing us to springboard our own regrets and disappointments.

Well worth a read – a collection not to be ignored.

*Agnes Meadows*

## Other poetry by Mary Pargeter

*Journey in Shades*
In this evocative collection, the poet writes with honesty of love, heartbreak and death and recollects a country childhood before the loss of innocence, reflecting with admirable frankness on those universal rites of passage common to us all.

Surrey Life magazine, Juliette Foster
*"This first volume of poems by Mary Pargeter is an exquisite feast of childhood memories, state of love and life reflections.*

*She writes with the lightness of petals falling on water yet underscoring the mildness is an honesty that surprises with its intensity.*

*Pargeter isn't afraid to wear her heart on her sleeve. Her openness is disarming, yet it's that very quality which gives Mary Pargeter's writing a lasting resonance."*

Guardian Books Online, Professor Carol Rumens
*"I have felt engaged with the work, and responsive to its emotional charge."*

Jay Ramsay, Poetry Editor, Caduceus Journal
*"She lets detail speak, often exquisitely, through things as they are; there is no attempt to escape through fantasy."*

ISBN
978-1-912031-08-5 (hardback)
978-0-9572970-4-3 (paperback)
978-0-9572970-3-6 (eBook)
978-0-9572970-2-9 (kindle)

www.ingramcontent.com/pod-product-compliance
Lightning Source LLC
Chambersburg PA
CBHW031457040426
42444CB00007B/1135